This book
belongs to

and I am ...
A Child of GOD !

Ark House Kids
PO Box 1722, Port Orchard, WA 98366 USA
PO Box 1321, Mona Vale NSW 1660 Australia
PO Box 318 334, West Harbour, Auckland 0661 New Zealand
arkhousekids.com

All bible verses are from the International Children Bible and the
Christian Standard Bible.

Cataloguing in Publication Data:
Title: The ABC Book For The Children Of God
ISBN: 978-0-6489912-1-2 (pbk.)
Subjects: CHILDREN; BIBLE RESOURCE; DEVOTIONAL;
Other Authors/Contributors: Wat, Jocelyn

Illustrated and designed by Jocelyn Wat

THE
ABC
❋━ BOOK ━❋

FOR THE
CHILDREN
━ ❯❯❯ of ❮❮❮ ━
GOD

FOR

The Children of God

SPECIAL THANKS TO

Mama & Papa
Granny & Grandad
Kennedy & Judy

Joshua, Joyce & William!

FOR YOUR ENDLESS
SUPPORT, PRAYERS AND LOVE!

A FOR ABBA!

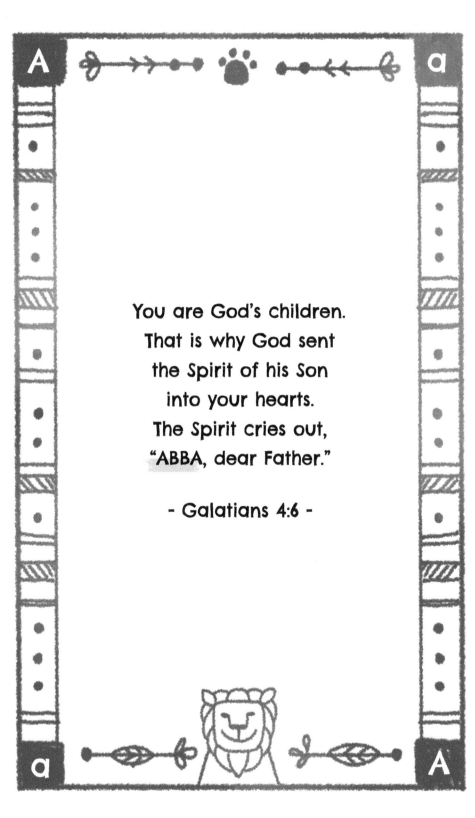

You are God's children.
That is why God sent
the Spirit of his Son
into your hearts.
The Spirit cries out,
"ABBA, dear Father."

- Galatians 4:6 -

B FOR BORN AGAIN!

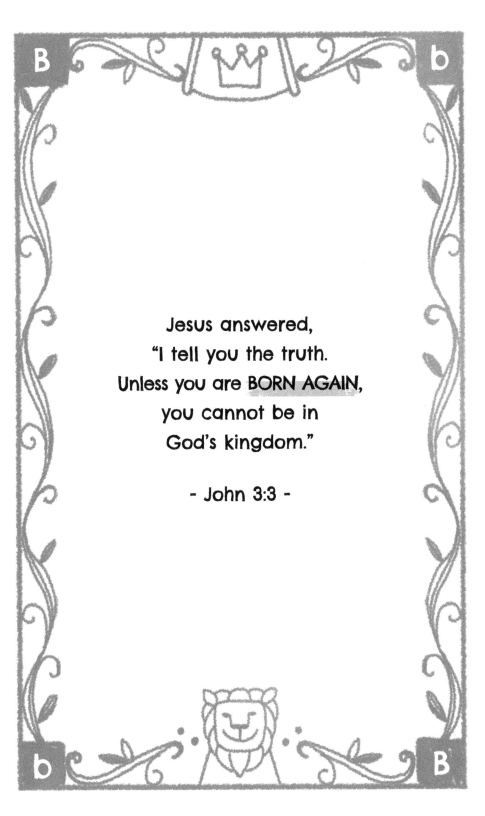

Jesus answered,
"I tell you the truth.
Unless you are BORN AGAIN,
you cannot be in
God's kingdom."

- John 3:3 -

C for Church!

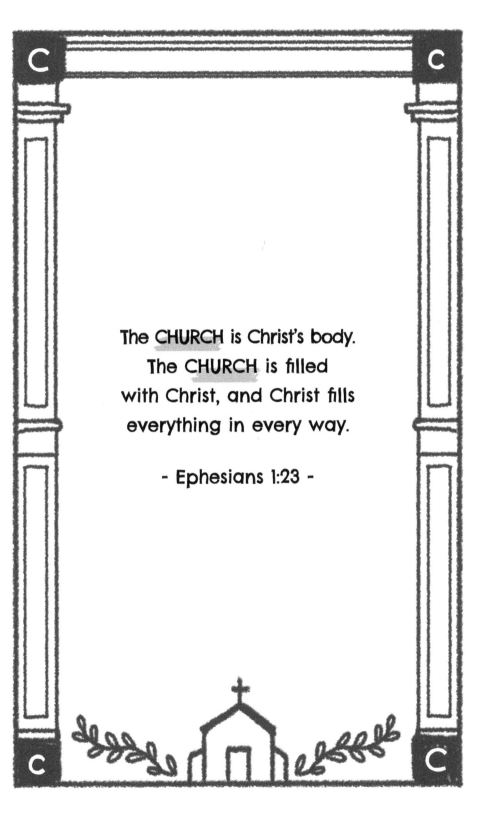

The CHURCH is Christ's body.
The CHURCH is filled
with Christ, and Christ fills
everything in every way.

- Ephesians 1:23 -

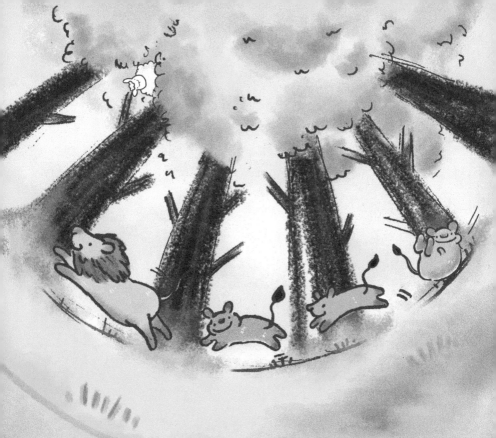

D

D FOR DESIRE!

Who do I have
in heaven but you?
And I DESIRE nothing
on earth but you.

- Psalm 73:25 -

E FOR ETERNAL LIFE!

"For God loved
the world so much that
he gave his only Son.
God gave his Son
so that whoever believes
in him may not be lost,
but have ETERNAL LIFE.

- John 3:16 -

F FOR FAITH!

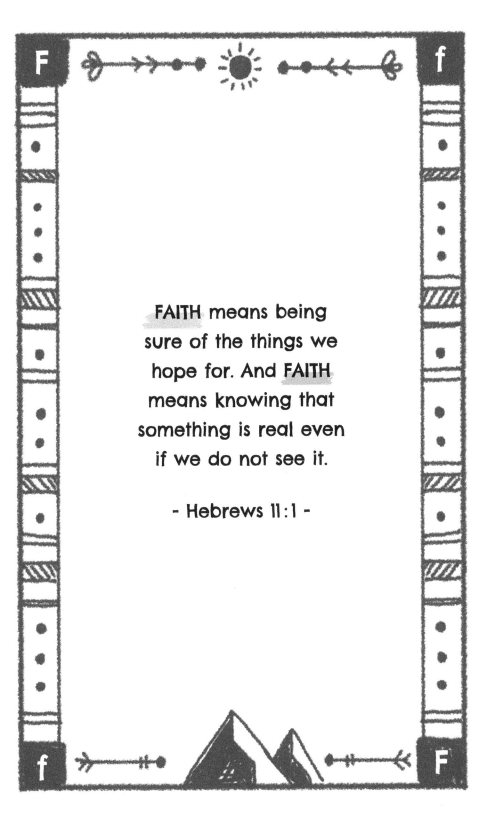

FAITH means being
sure of the things we
hope for. And FAITH
means knowing that
something is real even
if we do not see it.

- Hebrews 11:1 -

G FOR GLORY!

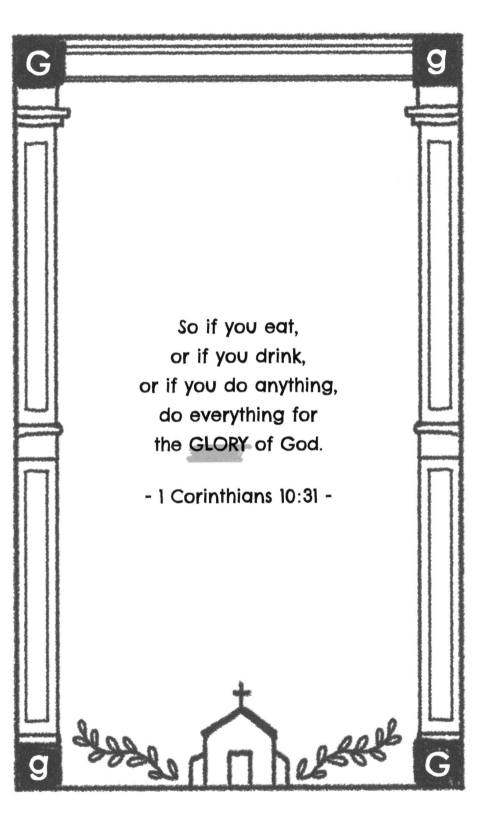

So if you eat,
or if you drink,
or if you do anything,
do everything for
the GLORY of God.

- 1 Corinthians 10:31 -

H FOR HEAVENS!

I look at the HEAVENS,
which you made with
your hands. I see the
moon and stars,
which you created.

- Psalm 8:3 -

I FOR INCENSE!

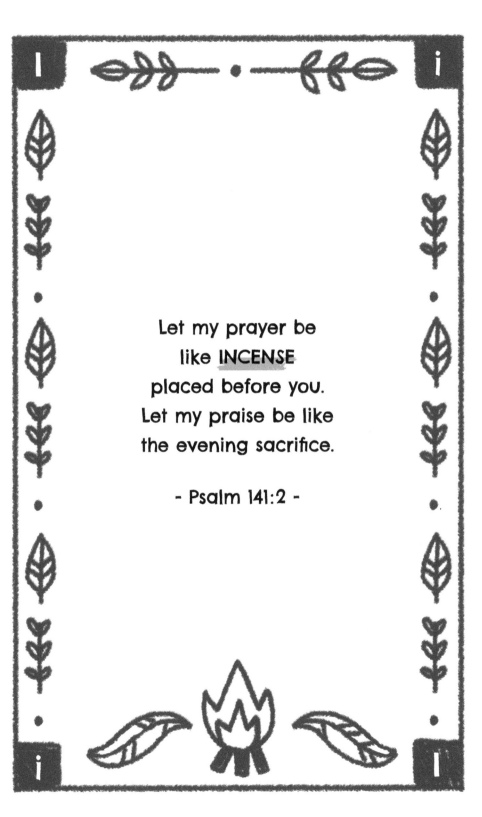

Let my prayer be
like INCENSE
placed before you.
Let my praise be like
the evening sacrifice.

- Psalm 141:2 -

J FOR JESUS!

This is how we know
what real love is:
JESUS gave his life for us.
So we should give our
lives for our brothers.

- 1 John 3:16 -

 K FOR KING!

God is **KING**
of all the earth.
So sing a song of
praise to him.

- Psalm 47:7 -

L FOR **LIGHT**!

The Lord is my LIGHT and
the one who saves me.
So why should I
fear anyone?
The Lord protects my life.
So why should I be afraid?

- Psalm 27:1 -

M FOR MAKER!

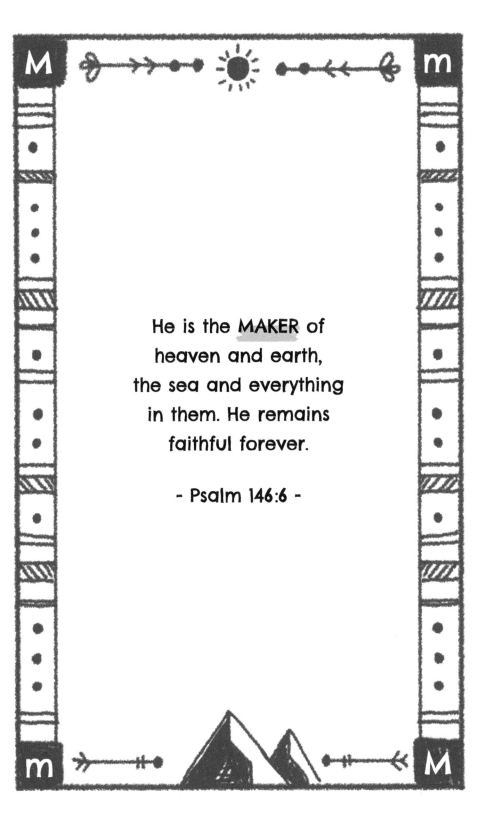

He is the MAKER of
heaven and earth,
the sea and everything
in them. He remains
faithful forever.

- Psalm 146:6 -

N FOR NEW!

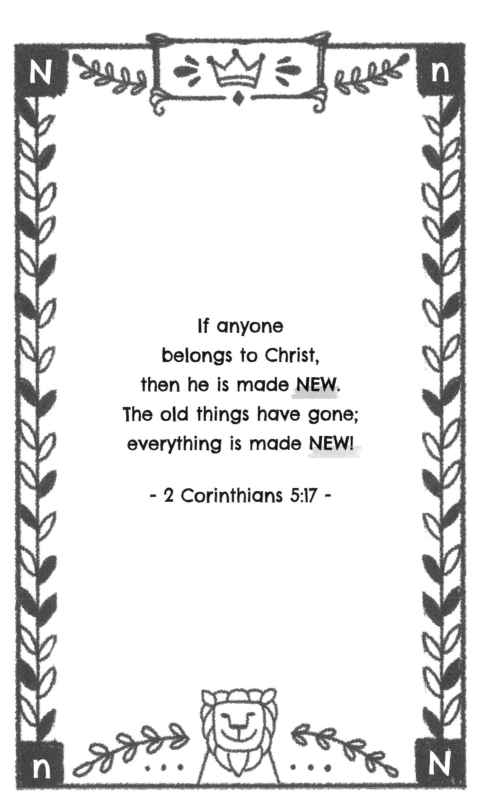

If anyone
belongs to Christ,
then he is made NEW.
The old things have gone;
everything is made NEW!

- 2 Corinthians 5:17 -

 O FOR OBEY!

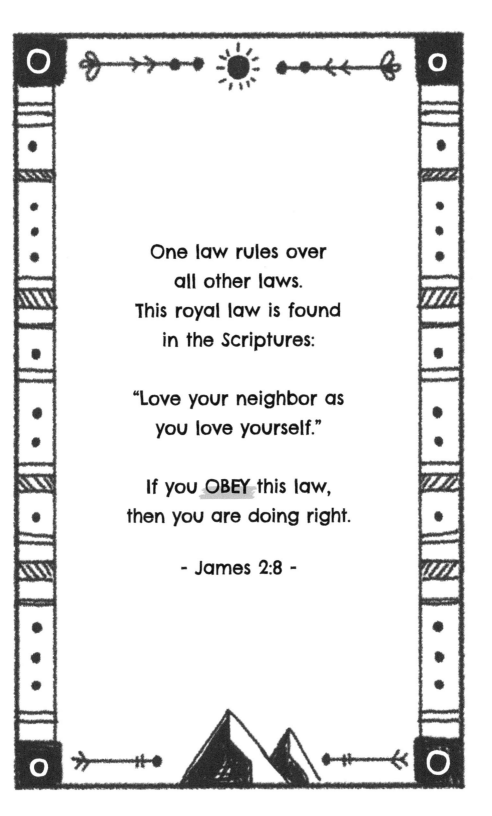

One law rules over
all other laws.
This royal law is found
in the Scriptures:

"Love your neighbor as
you love yourself."

If you OBEY this law,
then you are doing right.

- James 2:8 -

P FOR PRAY!

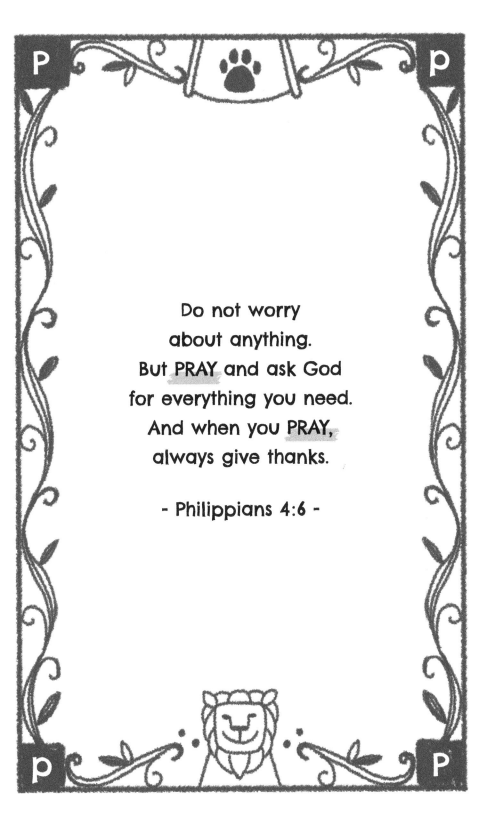

Do not worry
about anything.
But PRAY and ask God
for everything you need.
And when you PRAY,
always give thanks.

- Philippians 4:6 -

Q FOR QUIET!

The Lord your God
is with you.

The Mighty One
will save you.

The Lord will be
happy with you.

He will **QUIET** you
by his love.

He will sing and be
joyful about you."

- Zephaniah 3:17 -

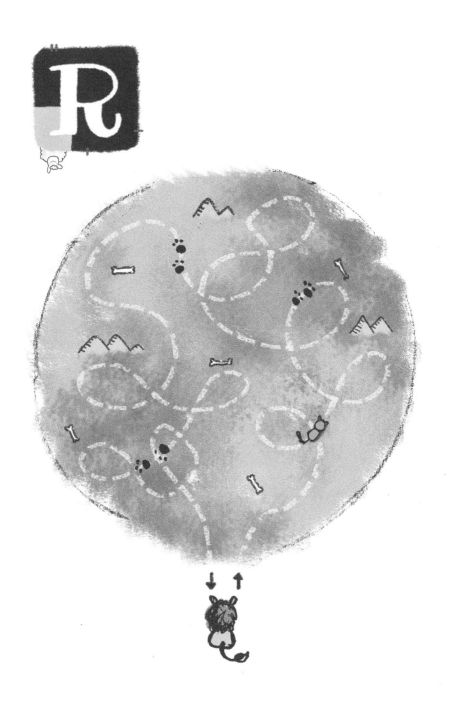

R FOR RETURN!

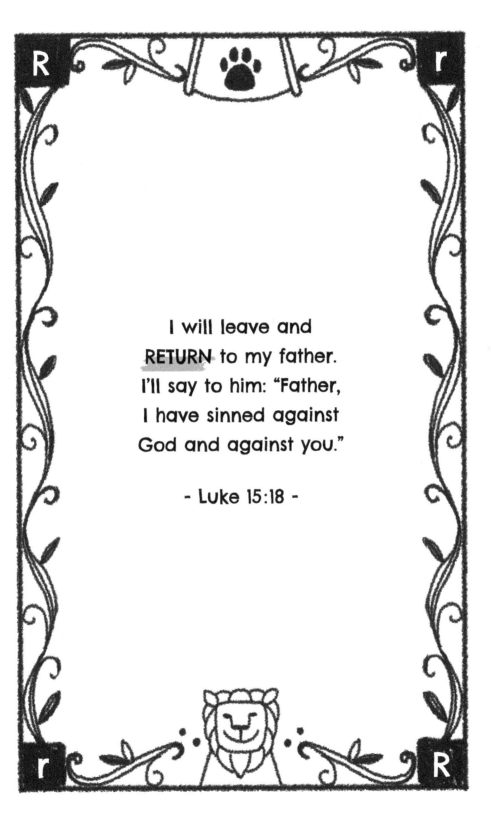

I will leave and
RETURN to my father.
I'll say to him: "Father,
I have sinned against
God and against you."

- Luke 15:18 -

S

S FOR SHEPHERD!

The Lord is my
SHEPHERD.
I have everything I need.
He gives me rest in
green pastures.
He leads me to
calm water.

- Psalm 23:1-2 -

T FOR TRUTH!

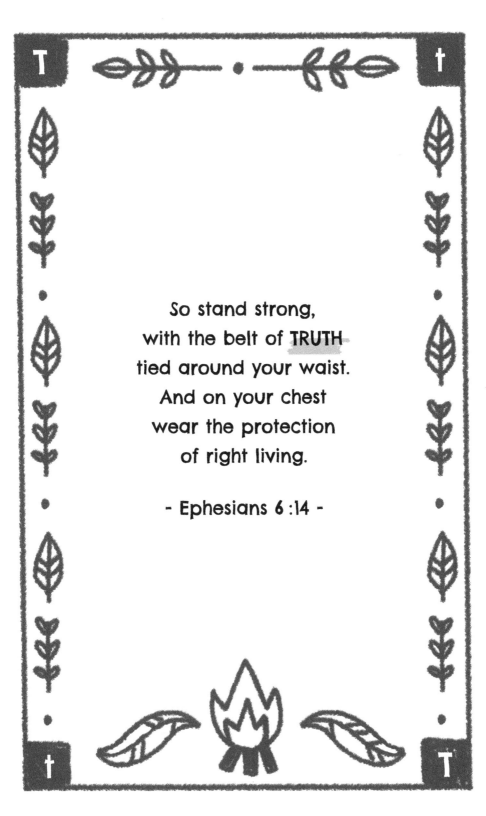

So stand strong,
with the belt of TRUTH
tied around your waist.
And on your chest
wear the protection
of right living.

- Ephesians 6 :14 -

U FOR UNITY!

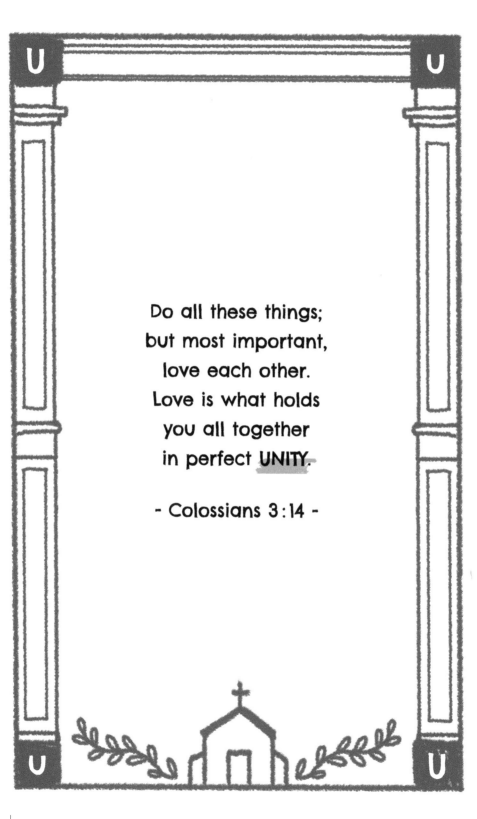

Do all these things;
but most important,
love each other.
Love is what holds
you all together
in perfect **UNITY**.

- Colossians 3:14 -

V FOR VINE!

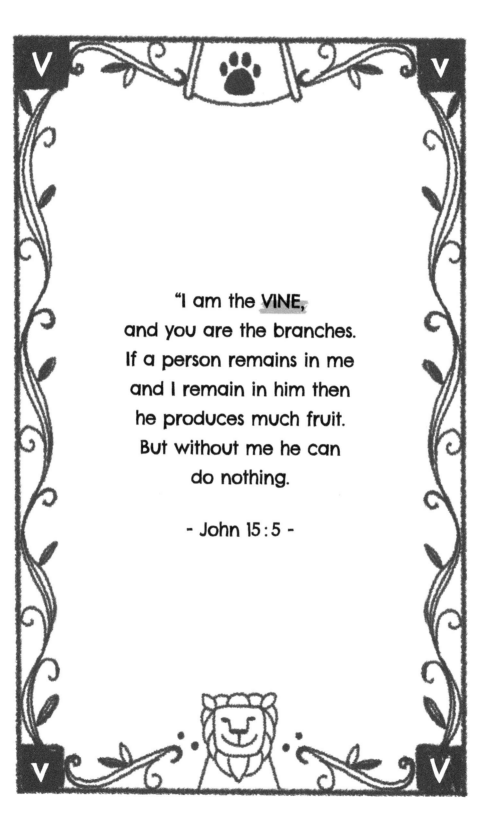

"I am the VINE,
and you are the branches.
If a person remains in me
and I remain in him then
he produces much fruit.
But without me he can
do nothing.

- John 15:5 -

W FOR WORSHIP!

My heart said of you,
"Go, WORSHIP him."
So I come to
WORSHIP you, Lord.

- Psalm 27:8 -

X for "Cross"!

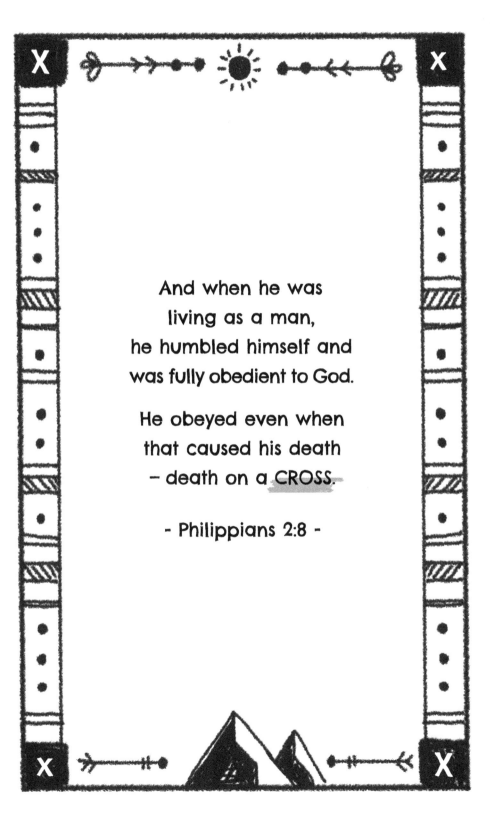

And when he was
living as a man,
he humbled himself and
was fully obedient to God.

He obeyed even when
that caused his death
– death on a CROSS.

- Philippians 2:8 -

Y FOR YOU ARE...

I said to the Lord,
"YOU ARE my Lord.
Every good thing
I have comes from you.

- Psalm 16:2 -

Z FOR ZION!

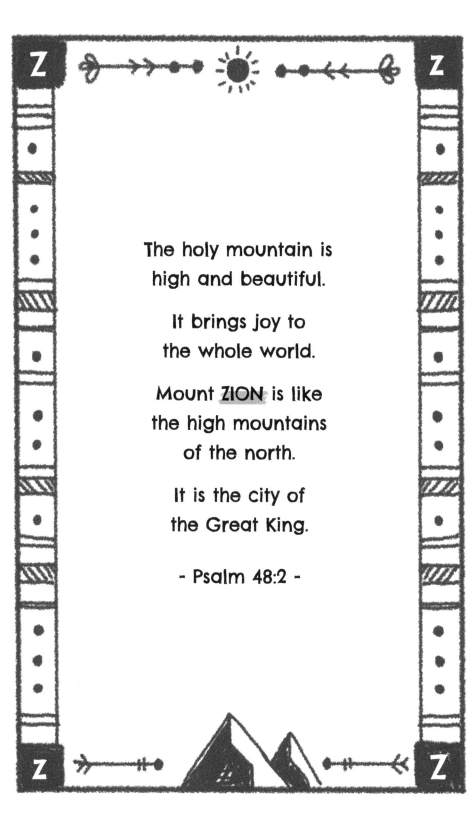

The holy mountain is
high and beautiful.

It brings joy to
the whole world.

Mount ZION is like
the high mountains
of the north.

It is the city of
the Great King.

- Psalm 48:2 -

MY PRAYER

Dear Heavenly Father,

I want to be a Child of yours.

I believe that Jesus had died on
the cross for our sins, and that
He had risen from the dead!
All because you love us dearly.

I long to love you too with all
my heart, will and strength!

In the name of Jesus,
AMEN!

FIND THE LOST SHEEPS!

THE GORGE
OF FAITH

THE ARK

THE PIER

LAND OF
TRAPS

THE VINEYARD

THE STONE
OF SACRIFICE

THE
WILD DESERT

THE FORBIDDEN
FOREST

?

THE BOOKS OF
THE BIBLE

A	Galatians	加拉太書	Gálatas	4.6
B	John	約翰福音	Juan	3:3
C	Ephesians	以弗所書	Efesios	1:23
D	Psalm	詩篇	Salmos	73:25
E	John	約翰福音	Juan	3:16
F	Hebrews	希伯來書	Hebreos	11:1
G	1 Corinthians	哥林多前書	1 Corintios	10:31
H	Psalm	詩篇	Salmos	8:3
I	Psalm	詩篇	Salmos	141:2
J	1 John	約翰一書	1 Juan	3:16
K	Psalm	詩篇	Salmos	47:7
L	Psalm	詩篇	Salmos	27:1
M	Psalm	詩篇	Salmos	146:6

IN DIFFERENT LANGUAGES

N	2 Corinthians	哥林多後書	2 Corintios	5:17
O	James	雅各書	Santiago	2:8
P	Philippians	腓立比書	Filipenses	4:6
Q	Zephaniah	西番雅書	Sofonías	3:17
R	Luke	路加福音	Lucas	15:18
S	Psalm	詩篇	Salmos	23:1-2
T	Ephesians	以弗所書	Efesios	6:14
U	Colossians	歌羅西書	Colosenses	3:14
V	John	約翰福音	Juan	15:5
W	Psalm	詩篇	Salmos	27:8
X	Philippians	腓立比書	Filipenses	2:8
Y	Psalm	詩篇	Salmos	16:2
Z	Psalm	詩篇	Salmos	48:2

ABOUT THE ILLUSTRATOR

Jocelyn Wat is an award-winning animator & illustrator based in Hong Kong. She aspires to use her art to encourage people, and as a creative channel for others to know more about our Creator!

CPSIA information can be obtained
at www.ICGtesting.com
Printed in the USA
BVHW021748280321
603603BV00004B/22